FOLK TALES FROM AROUND THE WORLD

Clever Manka

retold by Sharon Fear

The Boy and the Eagle
A Pima Folk Tale

retold by Christopher Keane

To Your Good Health
A Russian Tale

retold by Jan M. Mike

MODERN CURRICULUM PRESS

Pearson Learning Group

ISBN 1-4284-0399-X

Printed in the United States of America

5 6 7 8 9 10   V0N4   10 09

1-800-321-3106
www.pearsonlearning.com

FOLK TALES FROM AROUND THE WORLD

Contents

Clever Manka

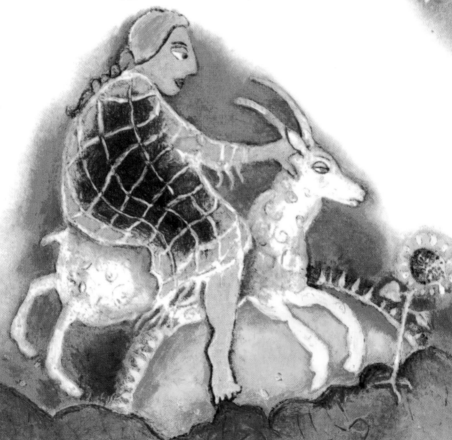

retold by Sharon Fear

illustrated by Mary King

Once there were two farmers working a piece of land together. They were digging and turning the earth, when what should turn up, but a cup made of gold! It was from olden times, and likely very valuable. They began to argue about who should have it.

"My hoe touched it first," said one.

"But certainly I saw it first," said the other.

"Yes, but I pulled it out of the ground!"

"Perhaps. But I. . . . "

This went on and on, until the only thing they could agree on was that they couldn't agree. They stood there scowling at each other. Someone else would have to settle the argument.

So they put the matter before the village judge. This judge was not at all certain how to decide. At last he told the two farmers that he would ask them three riddles. The one who came back the next morning with the best answers would have the gold cup.

The judge asked, "In all the world, what is the richest thing? What is the heaviest thing? And what is the swiftest thing?"

The first farmer went home. Feeling puzzled, he thought long and hard about the three riddles.

Finally he said to himself, "Why, it's not so hard. I know just what to say."

The other farmer went home too. He also was puzzled.

Now, this man had a clever daughter named Manka. When he told her about the riddles, she thought for a while. Then she thought for a while longer. Finally she told her father what answers he should give the judge the next day.

The next day, standing before the judge, the first man gave his answers.

"In all the world," he said, "the richest thing is the king. The heaviest thing is lead. And the swiftest thing is my bay mare, which can outrun any steed in the land."

Then the second man gave his answers, those suggested by his daughter.

"In all the world," he said, "the richest thing is the Earth. For out of the Earth comes everything we need. The heaviest thing is sorrow, which, when it comes, lies upon us heavier than stone. And the swiftest thing is the mind, for it can travel around the world in an instant."

The judge was very impressed by the second man's answers. He instantly awarded the gold cup to the man.

Then the judge looked at the man. "Tell me," he said. "Did you think of those answers by yourself? Or did you have help?"

The man admitted that he had a daughter named Manka who was uncommonly clever, and that she had told him what to say.

"I would like to meet this clever Manka," said the judge. "Will you bring her here tomorrow?"

And the man said, "Yes, certainly!"

When Manka and her father appeared the next day, a trial was in progress. Two brothers had inherited a farm when their father died.

Some of this farmland was rich and some of it was quite poor. The brothers could not agree how to divide it.

"Manka!" said the judge. "I hear you are uncommonly clever. How would you settle this dispute?"

Manka thought for a while.
Then she said that she would let
one brother divide the land and let
the other brother have first choice.

The brothers were more than
happy with this decision. And so
was the judge. He was also
delighted with Manka. She was
not only clever, but also had a very
pleasing manner.

After a time it came about that the judge wanted to marry Manka, and she wanted to marry him. Manka's father was happy at the prospect. But the judge's father had objections. After all, the judge was a man of power and privilege. Manka was only the daughter of a peasant.

The young judge told his father how clever Manka was.

"Very well," said his scowling father. "If she is so clever, let her do this. Ask her to come to you neither by day nor by night, neither walking nor riding, and neither clothed nor unclothed. If she can do that, you may marry."

Manka was told of these conditions. She thought for a while. Then she said to her father, "Bring me the goat from the pasture and a long length of fish net."

Early the next morning, long before sunrise, Manka arose. She wrapped herself in the fish net. Then she jumped on the goat's back and rode along with one foot dragging on the ground.

She arrived at the judge's house just at dawn, as the stars were beginning to fade. She had come to him neither by day nor by night, neither walking nor riding, neither clothed nor unclothed.

She had done all that the judge's father asked. He had no choice but to give his permission. Only one more thing stood in the way of the wedding.

"Just promise me this," said the judge to Manka. "You must never interfere with any of my judgments. If you disobey me in this, I will send you back to your father."

Manka promised. And so they were married and lived quite happily for a time.

Then two men came to court to determine which one owned a certain colt. At the trial it came out that both men had been in the marketplace at the same time. A mare belonging to one man had given birth under the other man's wagon. Now the owner of the wagon was claiming ownership of the foal.

Perhaps the judge was tired or thinking of something else at the time. At any rate, he said, "The owner of the wagon is, of course, the owner of the colt." And that was that.

The owner of the mare was angry at the unfairness of it. But what could he do? Then he remembered. The judge's wife was known to be kind as well as wise. He went to ask Manka for her help.

Manka didn't want to interfere. She remembered her promise to her husband. But his decision had been such a bad one. And this man was so downcast that she was moved to help him.

So she told him exactly what to do and what to say. "Only you must never, ever tell the judge that I'm the one who advised you," she said to the man.

The man promised.

That afternoon he sat down by the side of the road. He was holding a fishing pole. Its line dipped into a pail of water in front of him.

When the judge walked by, he recognized the man from that day's trial. The judge asked him what he was doing.

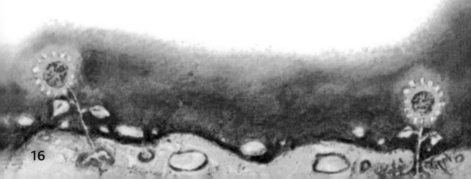

"Fishing," said the man.

The judge burst out laughing. He said, "You can't catch a fish in a pail of water!"

"If a wagon can give birth to a foal, I can catch fish in a pail," replied the man.

Suddenly the judge turned somber. "I see what you mean," he said. "The foal will be returned to you. I will see to it."

But something about this incident made the judge suspicious. He questioned the man. Finally the man admitted that, indeed, it was Manka who had instructed him.

The judge returned home. He was very angry. "You were a peasant's daughter," he said, scowling. "I made you my wife. I gave you a life of privilege. But, Manka, you have broken our agreement. You must leave!"

"As you wish," said Manka. "I will leave tomorrow for my father's house. I ask only one favor. Let me take with me my most beloved possession."

The judge was not a cruel man.

"You may take it, whatever it is," he replied.

That night was to be their last night together. Manka was very quiet. Together they ate her husband's favorite food and drink. He ate little, and he still seemed quite angry.

But behind his scowling face, Manka saw sadness. And when he went to sleep, Manka looked at him. He looked so gentle and kind. Manka realized he was a good man who had made a mistake. And she knew what she had planned was right.

For Manka knew that her husband often fell into a very deep sleep.

So when some time had passed, and he was deeply asleep, she called to the servants. Together they lifted up her husband. They carried him all the way to her father's house. There they put him to bed. And then they waited.

The judge slept the whole night through. When he awoke and looked about him, he was alarmed and confused. He called for his servants, None came. Then at last he called, "Manka! Manka!" And there she was at his bedside.

"Where am I? What has happened?" he asked her.

"Oh," she said, "you are in bed in my father's house. You told me to leave, and I have done so. You told me to take with me my most beloved possession, and I have done that also."

His face went red. First it was with shame at how foolish he had been, and then with embarrassed delight. He realized that he, himself, was Manka's most beloved possession.

"Manka," said the judge. "Come home with me. It is clear that you are far wiser than I am."

Manka thought for a while. She was angry to have been ordered from her home. But she was willing to forgive her husband. From that time forward, Manka and the judge lived as happily as two people can.

Manka was as clever as always. More and more people sought her wisdom. The judge seemed to gain in stature too. Everyone said his opinions were wiser, and his rulings more sound than before.

Those who knew Manka were sure they knew why.

The Boy and the Eagle
A Pima Folk Tale

retold by Christopher Keane
illustrated by Donna Perrone

In the shadow of a black mountain, near a desert stream, there once lived a Pima boy named Kelihi. As the oldest of five brothers and sisters, Kelihi had many chores. Too many, he sometimes thought!

He was responsible for helping his father grow cotton and corn. Beans and squash also needed his care. And in the desert, he hunted rabbits, quail, and lizards.

There was much to do every day, but twelve-year-old Kelihi wished for something more. He wished for adventure.

One day, while he was working in the field, a shadow passed over him. He looked up and saw an eagle. The eagle glided over the desert and sailed above the mountain. Kelihi imagined spreading his own wings and soaring above the cliffs. He wondered what it was like high on the mountain. Then he thought about the eagle's nest. He knew it was a great thing to find an eagle's nest.

"Father, I want to climb the mountain and look for an eagle's nest," he said.

"That isn't easy," his father said. "The mountain is a hard obstacle to climb. And you have to be lucky enough to find a nest."

"But *you* did it," said Kelihi.

His father smiled. "Yes, but I went with my father, who taught me much about the eagle. That is our tradition. Someday, when you are older, I will go with you too."

"I'll be older tomorrow," said Kelihi.

His father laughed. "Not tomorrow. It's harvest time. I need your help with the beans and the corn."

Kelihi stomped away, disappointed.

"Beans and corn," grumbled Kelihi. "Eagles are more meaningful—much more important than beans and corn! Why must I wait?"

Kelihi decided not to wait.

The next morning, Kelihi awoke before dawn. He moved quietly so that he would not wake his family. He packed cornbread and dried meat into a leather pouch. He filled a gourd with cool water and then slung the hollowed-out squash over his back. Then he left, leaving his family sleeping in the ramada, the open structure close to the house. Finally he headed toward the mountain.

Kelihi walked for many hours. Rabbits scurried among the cactus. Lizards darted up the mesquite trees. At last, he came to the foot of the mountain. Looking up, he saw the high cliffs where the eagles lived. Slowly Kelihi began to climb.

Kelihi climbed carefully. The day was very hot. Sweat dripped from his long black hair. The rocks felt like hot coals under his fingers. But Kelihi continued up the side of the mountain.

Near the top, he came to a steep cliff. He struggled up the smooth rock. His muscles ached and his legs shook. Finally, Kelihi overcame all these discomforts and stood at the top. There he sang a loud song of victory. Kelihi looked to the desert far below and felt he could see the whole world. His family's home and fields were tiny specks.

Kelihi searched the mountaintop. He searched trees, caves, and crevices, or cracks in the rock. Soon, he heard chirping and followed the sound. On a small ledge above a cliff was an eagle's nest. The chirping came from inside the nest.

Kelihi climbed to the ledge. Balancing on the edge, he looked into the nest and saw two baby eagles. Soft downy feathers covered their bodies. The two small eagles looked like fluffy little storm clouds—with tiny eyes.

The small birds shrieked at Kelihi as their mouths gaped with hunger.

Kelihi opened his pouch. He tore off bits of the dried meat and dropped them into the birds' mouths. The eaglets gulped the food and then cried for more.

Kelihi laughed to see the birds eat. He was happy, knowing he had found an eagle's nest. It was a great day.

Then he felt anxious as he began to think about his father. "I hope he will forgive me," Kelihi said aloud.

Then Kelihi looked back at the eaglets and longed to feel the downy feathers. So he reached for the closest bird. But *snap!* It pecked at his fingers. Startled, Kelihi slipped backward. Then in a flash, he fell from the ledge.

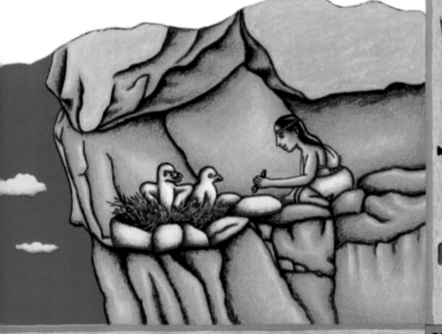

Kelihi tumbled down the cliff. He bounced over rocks. He fell through thorn bushes. Finally, he landed on a small ledge in the middle of a sheer cliff.

His hands were bruised. His knees were scraped. When he tried to rise, he found that his right ankle was too weak to support him. Kelihi knew he could climb no further. He sat on the ledge and looked all around. There was no way up and there was no way down.

Kelihi began to sob. "Why didn't I obey Father? Why did I sneak away?" he said. Now Kelihi was regretting his entire adventure on the mountain.

Then he caught his breath and tried to think of what his father might do if he were there.

"When you are in trouble," his father always said, "it is best to try to relax, stand back, and look at the problem. Then you will see things more clearly."

So Kelihi tried to relax and see things more clearly. He lay back on the smooth rock and closed his eyes. After a while, he fell asleep.

Kelihi dreamed of a huge eagle. The eagle glided down and landed beside him. It cocked its great head toward him and began to speak. Kelihi was startled when the eagle said his name.

"Kelihi, don't be surprised. In dreams, all animals speak," said the gigantic eagle.

The eagle continued, "I was watching you. The baby eagles are my children. I am responsible for their safety. I could never let you touch them."

"I'm sorry," answered Kelihi. "I never meant to harm them."

Then Kelihi promised he would respect the eaglets and he would never try to touch them again.

The eagle looked hard at Kelihi, and then told him to climb on its back. Kelihi pulled his bruised body onto the mighty bird. The feathers felt warm and tickled his skin. The eagle, spreading its wings and without looking back, soared off the ledge.

Kelihi gasped as the eagle swooped down. The wind breezed against his face as the eagle flew in huge circles. It flew past the cliffs and sailed over mountain streams. Then, gently, it landed in the desert near a prickly pear cactus. Amazed, Kelihi slid off the eagle's back. He sang his thanks and the great bird flew away.

Suddenly Kelihi woke up. He was still lying on his back and sighed when he realized he had only been dreaming. But when he sat up, he saw he was no longer on the mountain. He was in the desert, near his family's home.

Then he looked on the ground beside him and saw a tail feather of the great eagle. At that moment, Kelihi knew that his time with the eagle was not a dream. Only with the eagle's help could he have survived his fall and ended up near home.

As Kelihi walked home, he realized his body was healed. Not even his ankle hurt. When his worried mother and father saw him, they rushed to hug him. Then they scolded him for running off to find the eagle by himself.

"I'm so sorry," Kelihi moaned. "It was wrong not to obey you, Father. From now on, I will listen to you and I will have patience."

Then he pulled the giant eagle feather from his pouch and held it up in the gentle breeze.

His father looked at the feather and said, "There must, indeed, be a story to go with this feather. I can only imagine what you overcame to find it and bring it home. One thing I'm sure of is that now you understand more about the greatness of the eagle. And the importance of our traditions."

Kelihi looked at his father's strong, loving face. Then he took his father's hand and placed the great feather lightly on the open palm.

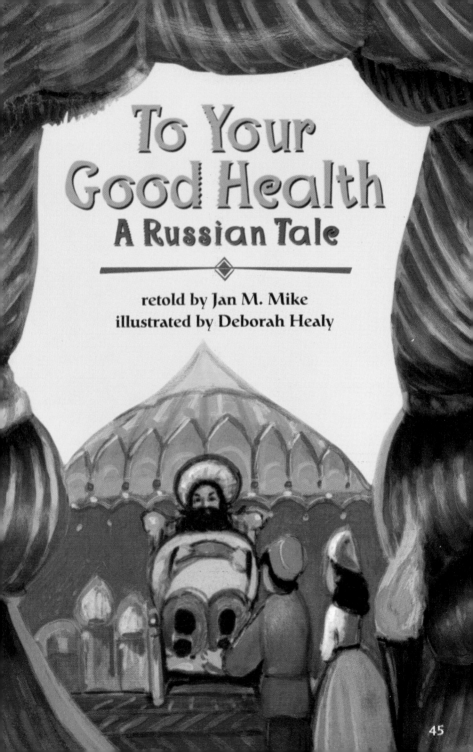

To Your Good Health
A Russian Tale

retold by Jan M. Mike
illustrated by Deborah Healy

Long ago in old Russia, there lived a young man named Pavel. As a child, he had been a shoemaker's apprentice, and now he owned a little shop.

Now I must tell you that there was nothing at all out of the ordinary about Pavel. Oh, he was brave and strong, and clever and handsome. His eyes were bright blue and alive with curiosity. He could sing and play the flute like a master, and he crafted shoes and belts that made rich men and women weep with admiration. But Pavel was an ordinary man.

One day, as Pavel worked in his shop, the bell above the door rang. He looked up with a start. Standing before him was the czar's only daughter, Larissa. The czar was the king. Pavel knew enough to respect his superiors, so he jumped to his feet and bowed.

The czar's daughter smiled and turned to look over his wares. As Larissa examined purses, shoes, gloves, and belts, Pavel looked at her.

I must tell you that there was nothing out of the ordinary about Larissa either. Oh, her black eyes sparkled with intelligence and wit. She could ride the wildest horse and speak seven languages. She could play instruments and sing like a nightingale. But except for those things, Larissa was a very ordinary young woman.

Pavel showed Larissa a pair of fine dancing slippers, blue velvet crusted with tiny pearls. She looked up at him. Her eyes sparkled. They seemed to say, "I find you interesting. I would like to know you better."

Pavel smiled, and his eyes seemed to answer, "I find you beautiful and clever. I too would like to know you better."

Now, since their mouths said nothing beyond the ordinary, no one but they knew what their eyes had agreed to. Larissa took the dainty, delicate slippers and left the store. But she returned the next day, and the next.

A year passed. Larissa now owned 183 pairs of new shoes, sixty-seven new purses, forty-eight new belts, and sixty-two pairs of new gloves. When her father, the czar, received the shoemaker's bill, he decided that something had to be done.

Everyone agreed that the czar was an extraordinary man. As large and hairy as a wintering bear, he had the flaming temper of a wild boar, or pig. Every day he would issue new orders that no one dared disobey. He ruled the land with fear and fury.

The czar decreed it was time for Larissa to be married. Princes from around the world arrived at the palace. Some were fat, and others thin. Some were tall, and others short. Each begged permission to marry her, and each, in turn, she refused. Eventually the flood of princes slowed to a trickle. Then it stopped.

Pavel realized it was now his turn. Larissa had turned down all his superiors. That must mean that her eyes spoke the truth. But how could he, a mere shoemaker, gain permission to marry the only daughter of the czar?

The czar had ordered many laws passed, but the most foolish one was this: Each time the czar sneezed, bells rang across the land. People everywhere had to drop what they were doing and shout, "To your good health!" Shoemaker and shepherd, farmer and shopkeeper, all had to stop and shout, "To your good health!"

As Pavel tried to think of a way to bring himself to the czar's attention, the sneezing bells rang. Everyone stopped and shouted, "To your good health!"

Everyone, that is, but Pavel.

Immediately people noticed, and soon the royal guards were upon him. They dragged him to the royal palace and brought him to the throne room.

Pavel bowed. The czar bristled with anger, but Larissa, who was standing next to him, smiled. Most men would have been terrified, but not Pavel. He saw a chance to make the czar notice him.

"Did you not hear the royal sneezing bells?" the czar asked.

"Yes, I heard the bells, Your Royal Highness," Pavel answered.

"Do you know the law?" the czar demanded.

"Yes, I know the law, Your Extreme Mightiness," Pavel replied.

"Then say it," the czar shouted. "Say 'To your good health!' "

Pavel threw back his shoulders, standing tall. Here was his chance.

"Certainly, Your Very Great Greatness! To my good health!"

The czar turned red with rage.

"Are you a fool?" he demanded.

"No, I am not, Your Very Majestic Majesty," Pavel answered, bowing once more.

Larissa giggled behind her fan.

"How dare you disobey my law! It is not to *your* good health, it is to *my* good health! To my good health!" The czar pounded his chest.

"Very well, Your High and Mightiness, to my good health! Mine!" Pavel replied, pounding his own chest.

The czar's high minister tiptoed up to Pavel. In a very loud whisper he said, "If you do not say what the czar wishes to hear, he will order you killed."

"I will gladly say what the czar wishes to hear," Pavel answered. "I vow it. But first he must give me permission to marry Larissa."

Larissa laughed out loud.

"Oh, yes, Father. I will marry him," she cried out.

The czar turned purple with fury.

"No, you won't!" he shouted. "Throw this man into the bear cage!"

As the guards hauled him across the palace, it was clear to Pavel that he had made the czar notice him. So far, so good. Now if he could just survive the bear cage, perhaps he could make the czar like him.

The guards opened a large iron gate. They threw Pavel into a small room. The floor was covered with dirt, and the walls were cold and slimy.

A low growl rumbled through the little room. Pavel looked up as a very large bear rushed at him. Pavel's eyes opened wide and the bear stopped suddenly. Pavel closed his eyes and heard the bear growl again. Pavel's eyes flew open, and the bear took a step back.

For some reason the animal would not attack as long as Pavel stared at it. To survive, he would have to stare at the bear all night long.

As darkness fell, Pavel's eyelids grew heavy. It had been an exciting day, and he was tired. He slapped at his cheeks, then pinched his elbows. He pulled his hair. He even bit his tongue. It was going to be a very long night.

Then he heard a voice, a sweet and lovely voice singing a loud, lively peasant tune. Larissa had sneaked out of bed. She was sitting next to the bear cage, singing.

"Do you often sing the bear to sleep?" Pavel asked.

"All the time," Larissa answered. "Why don't you sing with me?"

And so he did. All night long, Pavel and Larissa sang the loudest songs they knew. When dawn arrived, Larissa tiptoed away. Pavel stood and stretched, wide awake.

A few minutes later, the czar's high minister arrived. He looked quite surprised to see Pavel alive. Guards pulled the shoemaker from the bear cage. They gave him a crust of dry bread, a cup of warm water, and a rag to nap on. His liberty did not last, however. That evening they took him back to the czar.

The czar still looked angry as Pavel walked into the room. Larissa, sitting next to her father, winked at Pavel. He smiled at her.

"Well, young man," said the czar, "now you know how it feels to be close to death. Will you tell me what I wish to hear?"

"I'm not afraid of dying ten deaths, Your Most High and Mighty Excellence! I will say what you wish to hear only if you give me permission to marry Larissa."

"Oh, do give permission, Father," Larissa begged.

The czar ignored her. His cheeks were flaming with rage.

"How dare you disobey me when I issue an order? Ten deaths? I will show you ten deaths! Throw him into the boar pen."

The guards marched Pavel out of the room, down the hall, and past the bear cage. One guard opened a second iron gate and threw the shoemaker into the boar pen.

Ten wild boars crowded the little room, grunting and squealing. These were not sweet little pigs with pink skins and curly tails. They were huge, ferocious animals with sharp tusks and angry red eyes.

"Ten deaths," Pavel muttered. "Well, we'll see."

He grabbed his little silver flute out of his sleeve and began to play. Sweet music drifted upon the air.

The boars sniffed and snorted, squinting at the silver flute. Slowly, one boar stood on his hind legs and began to dance. Then another stood up, and another, until all the boars danced to the sound of the little silver flute.

Pavel wanted to laugh at the silly sight, but he knew if he took his mouth away from the flute, the boars would rush over to hurt him. An hour passed and his arms grew tired, but still he played.

"Well, this won't do at all."

Pavel looked up. Larissa stood outside the boar pen, holding her lute. He wanted to ask her what she meant, but he didn't dare stop playing.

"Here, let's try a faster tune," Larissa said, and she began to strum the lute's strings.

Pavel joined in, and as they played a lively tune, the boars began to dance even faster. Larissa and Pavel played for an hour or more, until all the boars collapsed in a snoring heap.

Larissa tiptoed off, carrying her lute. Pavel climbed to the top of the pile of snoring boars and fell fast asleep.

Early the next morning, the czar's high minister was quite surprised to find Pavel napping on a pile of exhausted boars. The guards woke him and dragged him from the cell, while the wild pigs continued to snore.

Once more Pavel was given bread and water. Since he wasn't tired this time, he spent the afternoon playing chess with the high minister. When evening came, the guards took him to the throne room.

The czar looked furious as Pavel walked into the room. Larissa, sitting next to her father, waved at Pavel. He grinned at her.

"Well," said the czar, "now you know how it feels to be close to ten deaths. Will you tell me what I wish to hear?"

"I'm not afraid of dying a hundred deaths, Your Extreme and Very Wise Excellence! I will say what you wish to hear only if you will give me permission to marry Larissa."

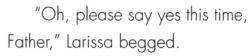

"Oh, please say yes this time, Father," Larissa begged.

The czar ignored her, his face red with fury.

"Once more you dare to disobey me when I issue an order. A hundred deaths? I will show you a hundred deaths! Throw him into the rat pit."

The guards marched Pavel out of the room, down the hall, past the bear cage and the boar pen. One guard opened a third iron gate and pushed the shoemaker into the rat pit.

Small furry rats nearly filled the little room. They climbed the walls and hung from the ceiling. The dim light reflected off their sharp teeth and claws.

"A hundred deaths!" Pavel muttered. "I have to learn to watch what I say."

He pulled out his flute, but the rats simply ignored him. As ten rats climbed up his left leg and twenty climbed up his right leg, Pavel kicked furiously. Two rats fell to his shoulders, clinging to his shirt. He tried to brush them away.

"Oh, the poor things look hungry."

Pavel looked over at the door, where Larissa stood holding a large picnic basket.

"I'm afraid that someone forgot to feed them," she continued, taking a large wheel of cheese out of the basket.

"I fear that you're right. May I help you?" Pavel asked.

She handed him two loaves of freshly baked bread, and they both set about feeding the rats.

An hour later, a hundred well-fed and happy rats dozed in a corner of the little room. Pavel and Larissa laughed as they ate cold chicken and the rest of the bread and cheese.

"Aha!"

Pavel looked up. There was the czar, standing over Larissa.

"I knew that someone was helping this disobedient young man! It was you, my daughter."

Pavel hastily stood and bowed. Larissa made a quick curtsey. "Father, don't be angry," she said. "I was simply feeding our guest."

For once the czar looked more thoughtful than angry. He pulled the key off the wall, and swung open the door.

"Come along, Pavel. You might as well come too, Larissa. I have thought of a way to get rid of this young man, once and for all."

Larissa followed the czar through empty halls lit by torches. Pavel trailed behind.

Finally they stopped in front of a golden door. The czar unlocked the door and opened it. Pavel and Larissa followed him inside.

The room was filled with treasure. Gold plates were stacked to the ceiling. Gold cups lined the walls. Diamond and ruby necklaces were piled in one corner, with sapphire and emerald bracelets in another. Huge teardrop-shaped pearls filled one chest and glittering rings were scattered on the floor.

"Here, young man. Take whatever you want, or take all of it. Simply tell me what I want to hear, and leave my daughter alone."

But Pavel shook his head. "I thank you for your kind offer, Your Most Generous Majesty. But all of the treasure in the world means less to me than a single hair on your daughter's head. You see, I love her."

"You love her! Well, why didn't you say that in the first place?"

The czar rubbed his eyes, then he pulled at his mustache. Finally he turned to his daughter.

"Well, my dear, do you love him? Is that why you keep helping him?"

"Yes, Father."

"And if I give you permission to get married," he looked up at Pavel, "will you promise to say what I want to hear?"

Pavel bowed, then he reached over and grabbed Larissa's hand. "Oh, yes. The very next time you sneeze, Your Majesty."

"Well, since you are willing to face a hundred deaths for her, and you won't give her up for all my treasure, and since you love her and she loves you, I suppose I must give you permission."

And so it came to be that Pavel and Larissa were married the very next day. The wedding was a small one, but the wedding feast was quite large.

Now I must tell you that the czar's cook was a very good cook except for one thing. She always used far too much pepper. So when she placed a large roast in front of the czar, and the czar took a long sniff, his nose began to twitch. Everyone sat quietly and watched as the czar's eyes watered and his whole face turned red. He sniffled. He snorted. Then he gave a huge, loud, royal sneeze.

Before the sneezing bells could ring, before anyone could say anything, Pavel leaped to his feet and shouted, "To your good health!"

And, I'm told, they all lived happily ever after.